Wild and Tame
Needlefelt Animals

The information in this book was originally published in the following title:
"FELT ZOO- GENMO DE TSUKURU CHIISANA DOBUTSU TACHI"
Copyright © 2008 by Saori Yamazaki
Originally published in Japanese language by Kawade Shobo Shinsha Ltd. Publishers
English translation rights arranged with Kawade Shobo Shinsha Ltd. Publishers through Timo Associates, Inc., Tokyo

Japanese Language Edition Staff:
Direction: Norie Matsunaga (Loftways Inc.)
Photography: Shoko Matsuda and Masaki Terada (Loftways Inc.)
Styling: Maki Muramatsu (Loftways Inc.)
Illustration: Junko Raiko

English language rights, translation & production by World Book Media, LLC
Email: info@worldbookmedia.com
Translator: Namiji Hatsuse
English Language Editor: Lindsay Fair
Designer: Michele L. Trombley

First Published in the United States of America in 2013 by KP Kraft, an imprint of F+W Media, Inc., 10151 Carver Rd., Suite #200, Blue Ash, OH 45242. (800) 289-0963. First edition.

DISTRIBUTED IN CANADA BY FRASER DIRECT
100 Armstrong Avenue
Georgetown, ON, Canada L7G 5S4
Tel: (905) 877-4411

DISTRIBUTED IN THE U.K. AND EUROPE BY F&W MEDIA INTERNATIONAL
Brunel House, Newton Abbot, Devon, TQ12 4PU, England
Tel: (+44) 1626 323200, Fax: (+44) 1626 323319
Email: enquiries@fwmedia.com

DISTRIBUTED IN AUSTRALIA BY CAPRICORN LINK
P.O. Box 704, S. Windsor NSW, 2756 Australia
Tel: (02) 4560 1600, Fax: (02) 4577 5288
E-mail: books@capricornlink.com.au

SRN: U8588
ISBN-10: 1-4402-3906-1
ISBN-13: 978-1-4402-3906-9

Printed in China
17 16 15 14 13 12 5 4 3 2 1

About the Author

Saori Yamazaki was first introduced to needlecrafts growing up in Japan. She learned to knit and sew from her great-grandmother. Since she began needlefelting in 2000, her work has gained popularity and she regularly contributes to magazines and television shows. Saori enjoys working with wool, felt, and hand-woven materials at her studio in the foothills of the Yatsugatake Mountains. To learn more about Saori Yamazaki, visit her website at: www.atelier-charmys.com.

Wild and Tame Needlefelt Animals

24 Adorable Animals to Needlefelt with Wool

Saori Yamazaki

Contents

Getting Started

Author Note. 5
Tools and Materials 6
Needlefelting Basics. 8
Needlefelting Techniques for Animals 10

Projects and Instructions

Rabbit. 16
Red Panda 20
Prairie Dog 24
Sheep 28
Cat 32
Donkey 36
White Tiger 40
Ducks 44
Pig 50
Hippopotamus 54
Chipmunk 58
Brown Bear 62
Giant Panda. 66
Elephant 70
Owl 74
Paddybird 78
Goat 82
Green Frog 86
Chimpanzees 90
Giraffe 96
Lions 100
Brussels Griffon 106
Emperor Penguins .110
Kangaroos 116

Author Note

Needlefelting has always possessed an air of mystery for me. Just think about it for a minute: you use a funny-looking little needle to poke a fuzzy clump of wool and it magically transforms into a useful piece of felt. I found needlefelting so intriguing, that I simply had to try it out.

For my first foray into the fascinating world of needlefelting, I made a miniature version of my beloved dog. Upon examining my handiwork, I was astonished by how realistic the felted version looked. I was able to capture all of the essential details in wool—right down to his fluffy fur! From that moment, I was hooked on needlefelting and I couldn't wait to try my hand at recreating all of my favorite animals.

I've been an animal lover since childhood—even now as an adult, I make frequent visits to the zoo. Animals may not speak the same language as humans, but they have their own special way of communicating. When I observe animals, I can't help but imagine the conversations they have with each other. I picture two playful chipmunks competing to gather the most acorns or a doting mother teaching her ducklings to swim.

When needlefelting, my goal is always the same: create animals that convey the same magical expressions and personalities as their living, breathing counterparts. If you find that these little felted creatures embody the spirit of their real live inspirations, I will feel successful as an artist. I hope you enjoy creating your own felted friends!

—*Saori Yamazaki*

Tools and Materials

Needlefelting is a great craft to learn because it doesn't require a lot of fancy equipment or expensive materials. In fact, all you need is a needle and some wool in order to get started. The following guide defines the basic tools and materials necessary for creating the projects in this book and offers suggestions of other items that you might find useful on your felting journey.

Basic Tools

Felting needle: Use this special needle, which has tiny barbs that tangle the wool fibers, to create felt. Felting needles are available in a wide variety of shapes and sizes, including ones with handles that offer a comfortable grip.

Mat: Always position your wool on top of a mat when felting. The mat absorbs the needle as it is inserted into the wool, which protects your work surface and prevents the needle from breaking. Special needlefelting mats are available at craft stores, but you can also use high-density foam.

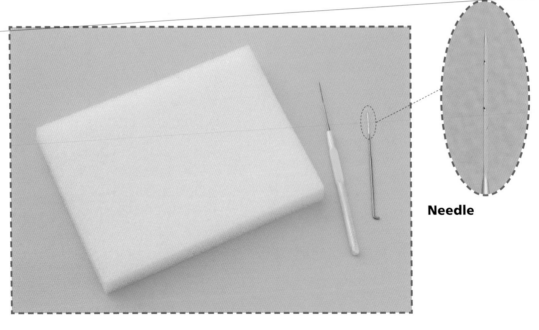

Needle

Mat

Additional Tools

Digital scale: The amount of wool roving required for each project is listed by weight in grams. Use a digital scale to measure out the exact amount of wool you need for your project.

Pliers: Use pliers for a better grip when attaching eyes, which are quite small and can be difficult to hold.

Scissors: Use a sharply pointed pair of scissors for cutting small pieces of wool roving to add details such as facial features and manes.

Doll needles: Use these extra-long needles specially designed for making stuffed toys when attaching eyes.

Thimble: You may want to use thimbles to protect your fingers when needlefelting.

Materials

Wool roving: All of the projects in this book use wool roving, which is spun wool that has been washed, combed and carded into long ropes, and sometimes dyed. A few of the projects call for uncarded wool in order to achieve a more natural, realistic look when adding details such as fur. Wool roving is widely available at craft stores. You can find uncarded wool online, or even directly at a farm.

Eyes: Many of the projects call for plastic eyes. These are available in a variety of sizes, shapes, and colors.

Wire: Some of the designs start with a wire frame, which allows an animal to stand upright. Floral wire is ideal for creating the frame and is available at craft stores, discount stores, and online.

Wool roving

Needlefelting Basics

Needlefelting is a technique that transforms wool fibers into a piece of non-woven cloth called felt. This process requires the use of a special felting needle, which is filled with tiny barbs (see page 6). When the needle is repeatedly inserted into the wool, the barbs catch the wool fibers, causing them to become tangled. The more the wool is felted, the more tangled the fibers become, which makes the piece of felt denser and smaller.

How Do I Separate the Wool Roving?

Wool roving is often sold in small balls. For each project, you will need to separate the necessary amount of wool roving from the ball before you can get started felting. The following guide shows the correct and incorrect ways to separate wool roving.

DO

DON'T

1. Hold the wool roving in two hands. Position each hand about 4" (10 cm) from the point where you want to separate the wool roving.

2. Gently pull to separate the wool roving. Make sure to keep the wool level as you are pulling.

Don't hold your hands close together when you pull the wool roving. This will exert too much pressure and cause the fibers to break apart unevenly.

How Do I Mix the Wool Roving?

Some of the designs require you to mix different colors of wool roving in order to create a realistic shade that is closer to an animal's actual coloring. Follow the steps below to mix different colors of wool roving.

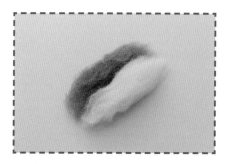

1. After separating the necessary amount of each color, align the tufts of wool roving side-by-side.

2. Hold the wool roving in two hands and gently pull to break it into two pieces.

3. Overlap the two pieces. Continue breaking the wool apart and realigning it until the colors are thoroughly mixed.

Needlefelting Techniques for Animals

This guide provides step-by-step instructions for the pig, which is shown on page 50. However, the same basic techniques apply to all of the animals in this book.

How to Needlefelt

Position the wool roving on the mat and hold it in place. Hold the felting needle in your dominant hand, just like you would hold a pencil. Insert the needle straight into the surface of the wool, being careful not to stick your fingers. Make sure not to insert the needle at an angle as this may cause it to break. Continue lifting and inserting the needle into the wool. This process causes the wool fibers to tangle and creates felt.

Make the Body

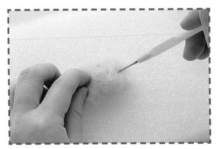

1. Layer a few pieces of wool on top of each other to create a tuft. Roll the tuft into the shape noted in the specific project instructions.

2. Felt the surface to keep the wool in place and roughly shape the body.

3. Add more wool as necessary, then felt to shape the body into the finished size noted in the project diagram.

Make the Legs

4. For each leg, roll a small tuft of wool into the shape noted in the project instructions. Felt one end of the leg, leaving the fibers loose at the other end for attaching to the body.

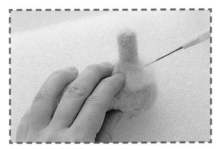

5. Attach each leg by felting the loose fibers to the body. Add a bit more wool to the attachment, then felt to create a smooth, uniform look.

Most of the animals have straight, cylindrical legs, just like in these photos. However, a few of the animals are designed in a sitting position, so their back legs look more like haunches. To create haunches, simply wrap wool around the top of the cylinders before attaching to the body.

Make the Head

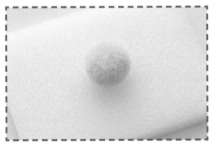

6. Roll a small tuft of wool into the shape noted in the specific project instructions. Felt the head into the desired shape and size.

7. Roll tiny tufts of wool between your fingertips to form the nose and mouth into the shapes noted in the specific project instructions. Felt to attach the nose and mouth to the head.

You may find it easier to add facial details such as the nose, mouth, and ears before the head is attached to the body. Adding the details first often allows you more room to work than when the head is already connected to the body.

Join the Head and Body

8. Position a small tuft of wool on the body at the point to attach the head. Lightly felt the center of the tuft to attach it to the body.

9. Align the head with the tuft of wool and felt to attach the head and body.

Finish the Body

10. Add more wool to give certain areas of the body a rounded shape, such as the rear end.

Make the Ears

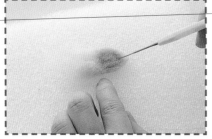

Many animals are designed with small ears composed of just one color of wool. This type of ear can be shaped as it is felted to the head.

11. Roll small tufts of wool between your fingertips to form the ears into the shape noted in the project instructions. Felt, leaving the fibers loose at one end. For ears made with two colors of wool, layer bits of the second color of wool on top of each ear and felt, concentrating your felting at the center to create a curved shape. Attach each ear by felting the loose fibers to the head.

Finish the Nose and Mouth

12. For noses and mouths made with two colors of wool, add bits of the second color of wool, then felt to attach. For the nose, use your needle to make two small holes for the nostrils.

Make the Tail

Finish

13. Roll a small tuft of wool into the shape noted in the project instructions. Felt one end, leaving the fibers loose at the other end. Attach the tail by felting the loose fibers to the body. Add a bit more wool, then felt to hide the attachment (refer to page 14).

14. Curl the tail using your finger. Felt to secure the curl in place.

15. Sew the eyes to the head (refer to page 15).

Special Techniques

A few of the projects use special techniques to add unique details to the designs. These techniques aren't complicated, but they will make a big difference in the finished appearance of your project.

Creating a Wire Frame

This technique uses floral wire to create a frame for four-legged animals, such as the donkey. The wire frame acts as a backbone, allowing the finished animal to stand without tipping over.

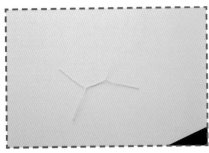

1. Twist two wires together at the center, leaving the ends free.

2. Fold the wire ends to form an H-shape. Trim the wire ends to the desired length.

3. Cover the wire ends with wool, then felt to attach.

4. Once the wire ends are completely covered, bend into shape until the frame can stand on its own.

5. Wrap a tuft of wool around the center of the wire frame and felt into shape.

Using a wire frame has several advantages. First, it's great for larger, heavier designs because the wire adds support. Second, a wire core makes the limbs more flexible and allows you to pose your animal more freely.

Hiding Attachments

This finishing technique is used to hide the area where two separate pieces have been attached. It is especially useful when the pieces being attached are two different colors, such as the panda's ear and head; however, it also works well for attaching pieces that are the same color.

1. Felt to attach the two pieces, such as the ear and head.

2. Cover the attachment with a small tuft of wool in the main color and felt.

Don't forget to hide your attachments! This little trick will give your finished projects a professional look.

Inserting Wool Strips

This process involves setting strip of wool into a piece that has already been felted. The strips will be attached at the base only. This method is ideal for creating long, fluffy areas of wool, such as the donkey's mane.

1. Cut a tuft of wool into a couple of small strips. Fold each strip in half and twist it together along the base using your fingertips.

2. Use a felting needle to insert the twisted section of the wool into the felted piece.

3. Trim the excess wool using scissors.

Sewing Eyes

Many of the animals in this book call for plastic eyes that are sewn to the felted animal. When sewing the eyes on, use thread in a color that coordinates with the animal you are making.

1. Hold the eye using a pair of pliers. Insert the thread through the shank. Insert the thread through the eye of a doll needle.

2. Insert the needle through the animal at the position to attach the eye.

3. Draw the needle out on the underside of the animal. Reinsert the needle through the animal and draw it out on the head. Repeat steps 2-3 until the eye is securely attached. Draw the needle out on the underside of the animal and knot. Cover the knot with felt.

Rabbit

Rabbit

Materials (for one rabbit)

Wool roving:
- 15 g of light gray, dark gray, or black wool
- Small amount of light pink wool
- Small amount of black wool

Eyes:
- Two 4 mm diameter black eyes

Instructions

Refer to pages 10–15 for a step-by-step photo reference of general felting and assembly techniques.

1. Body: Roll a tuft of wool into a cylinder. Felt to shape the body until it is 5½" (14 cm) around the middle. Add wool to the rabbit's rear end and felt into a rounded shape.

2. Head: Roll a tuft of wool into a cone and felt into shape. Join the head and body, **as shown on page 12**.

3. Legs: Roll small tufts of wool into four thin cylinders. For the back legs, felt one end of each leg, leaving the fibers loose at the other end (**refer to page 11**). For the front legs, felt one end of each leg, rounding slightly to create a foot, but leave the fibers loose at the other end. Attach the legs by felting the loose fibers to the body (**refer to page 11**).

4. Tail: Felt a small tuft of wool to the rabbit's rear end.

5. Ears: Roll small tufts of wool into two thin cylinders. Felt to shape the ears, leaving the fibers loose at one end. Layer a bit of pink wool on top of each ear and felt, concentrating the felting at the center to create a curved shape. Attach ears by felting the loose fibers to the head (**refer to page 12**).

6. Nose: Roll a tiny ball of black wool between your fingertips. Felt to attach the nose to the head.

7. Eyes: Sew a black eye on each side of the head (**refer to page 15**).

Tip:

When making the
body, add a bit more
wool to give the
rabbit's rear end a cute,
rounded shape.

Project Diagram

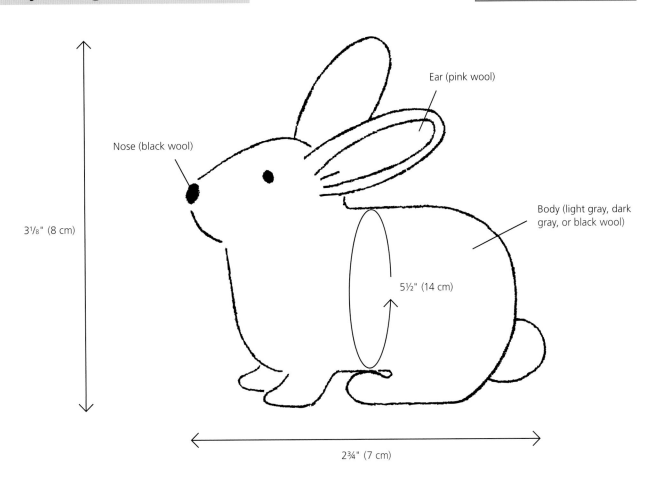

Nose (black wool)

Ear (pink wool)

Body (light gray, dark gray, or black wool)

3⅛" (8 cm)

5½" (14 cm)

2¾" (7 cm)

Red Panda

Red Panda

Materials

Wool roving:
- 25 g of reddish brown wool
- 10 g of brown wool
- Small amount of undyed wool

Eyes:
- Two 6 mm diameter black eyes

Instructions

Refer to pages 10–15 for a step-by-step photo reference of general felting and assembly techniques.

1. Body: Roll a tuft of reddish brown wool into a cylinder. Felt to shape the body until it is 5 ¼" (13.5 cm) around the middle.

2. Head: Roll a tuft of reddish brown wool into a ball and felt into shape. Join the head and body, **as shown on page 12**.

3. Underside: Felt brown wool to the underside of the neck and body.

4. Front Legs: Roll small tufts of brown wool into two thick cylinders. Felt one end of each leg, rounding slightly to create a foot, but leave the fibers loose at the other end. Attach the front legs by felting the loose fibers to the body (**refer to page 11**).

5. Back Legs: Roll small tufts of brown wool into two cylinders. Felt one end of each leg, rounding slightly to create a foot, but leave the fibers loose at the other end. Wrap a bit of reddish-brown wool around the top of each leg and felt to attach. Attach the back legs by felting the loose fibers to the body (**refer to page 11**).

6. Tail: Roll a small tuft of reddish brown wool into a thickly curved cylinder. Felt one end of the tail, leaving the fibers loose at the other end. Felt to attach the loose fibers of the tail to the body (**refer to page 13**). To add the stripes, insert five thin strips of undyed wool into the tail, then felt to attach (**refer to page 15**). Felt brown wool to the tail tip.

7. Ears: Layer small pieces of brown wool on top of each other and felt both sides, folding the edges in to form triangles. Leave the fibers loose at one end of each ear. Layer a bit of undyed wool on top of each ear and felt, concentrating the felting at the center to create a curved shape. Attach ears by felting the loose fibers to the head (**refer to page 12**).

8. Nose and Mouth: Roll a small tuft of undyed wool into a ball, then felt to attach to the head. To make the nose tip, roll a tiny ball of brown wool between your fingertips, then felt to attach to the nose. For the mouth, use your needle to make a thin indentation on the undyed felt.

9. Facial Details: Insert thin strips of wool into the head, then felt to attach. Use undyed wool around the eyes, cheeks, and ears and brown wool around the nose.

10. Eyes: Sew black eyes to the head (**refer to page 15**).

refer to page 15

Tip:

Make the tail and legs thick to replicate the red panda's bushy fur.

Project Diagram

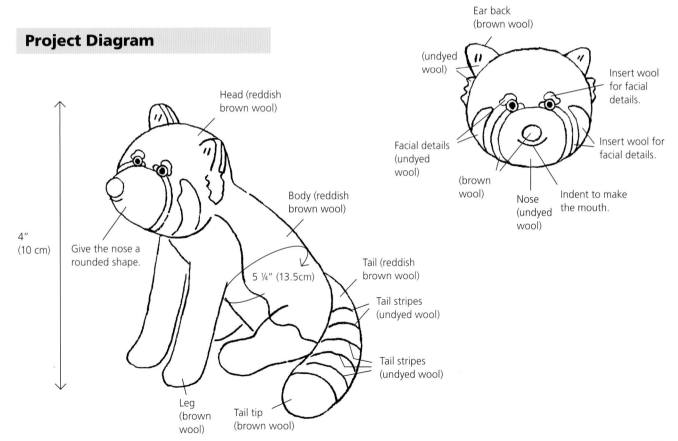

4" (10 cm)

Head (reddish brown wool)

Give the nose a rounded shape.

Body (reddish brown wool)

5 ¼" (13.5cm)

Tail (reddish brown wool)

Tail stripes (undyed wool)

Tail stripes (undyed wool)

Leg (brown wool)

Tail tip (brown wool)

Ear back (brown wool)

(undyed wool)

Insert wool for facial details.

Facial details (undyed wool)

Insert wool for facial details.

(brown wool)

Nose (undyed wool)

Indent to make the mouth.

Prairie Dog

Prairie Dog

Materials

Wool roving:
- 20 g of undyed wool
- Mixed wool: 5 g of light brown wool + 5 g of reddish brown wool
- Small amount of brown wool

Eyes:
- Two 6 mm diameter black eyes

Instructions

Refer to pages 10–15 for a step-by-step photo reference of general felting and assembly techniques.

1. Prepare Wool: Mix the light brown and reddish brown wool, **as shown on page 9**.

2. Body: Roll a tuft of undyed wool into a cylinder. Felt to shape the body. Add wool to the lower body and felt until it is 6 ¼" (15.5 cm) around the middle.

3. Head and Ears: Roll a tuft of undyed wool into a cone and felt into shape. For the ears, felt small tufts of the mixed wool to the head, concentrating the felting at the center to create a curved shape. Join the head and body, **as shown on page 12**.

4. Arms: Roll small tufts of the mixed wool into two thin cylinders. Felt one end of each arm, leaving the fibers loose at the other end. Attach the arms by felting the loose fibers to the body. Add wool to each attachment and felt into a rounded shape (**refer to page 12**).

5. Legs: Roll small tufts of the mixed wool into two balls. Felt one end of each leg, leaving the fibers loose at the other end. Attach the legs by felting the loose fibers to the body (**refer to page 11**).

6. Tail: Make the tail, **as shown on page 73**, using the mixed wool for the tail and brown wool for the tip. Felt to attach the tail to the body (**refer to page 13**).

7. Fur: Felt mixed wool to the head and body, leaving the undyed wool on the underside of the body visible.

8. Nose and Mouth: Roll a tiny ball of brown wool between your fingertips. Felt to attach the nose to the head. For the mouth, felt two thin strips of brown wool to the head, directly beneath the nose. Use your needle to make an indentation.

9. Eyes: Sew black eyes to the head (**refer to page 15**).

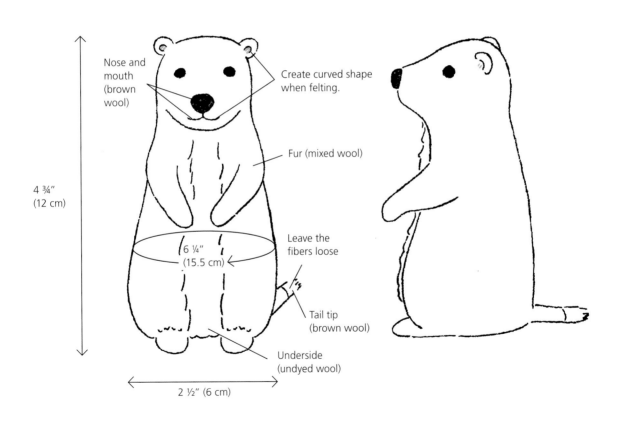

Nose and mouth (brown wool)

Create curved shape when felting.

Fur (mixed wool)

4 ¾" (12 cm)

6 ¼" (15.5 cm)

Leave the fibers loose

Tail tip (brown wool)

Underside (undyed wool)

2 ½" (6 cm)

Sheep

Sheep

Materials (for one sheep)

Wool roving:
- 20 g of undyed wool
- Small amount of black wool

Uncarded wool:
- 7 g of undyed, uncarded wool

Wire:
- Two 9 ¾" (25 cm) long pieces of floral wire

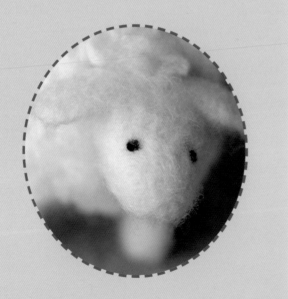

Instructions

Refer to pages 10–15 for a step-by-step photo reference of general felting and assembly techniques.

1. Body: Make the wire frame, **as shown in the diagram on the opposite page**. Cover the legs with undyed wool, then felt to attach (**refer to page 13**). Wrap a tuft of undyed wool around the center of the wire frame. Felt to shape the body until it is 6 ¼" (16 cm) around the middle.

2. Head and Ears: Roll a tuft of undyed wool into an oval and felt into shape. For the ears, felt small tufts of undyed wool to the head, concentrating the felting at the center to create a curved shape. Join the head and body, **as shown on page 12**.

3. Eyes: For open eyes, roll two tiny balls of black wool between your fingertips and felt to attach to the head. For closed eyes, felt two thin strips of black wool to the head.

4. Fleece: Insert tufts of uncarded, undyed wool into the body and felt to attach, leaving only the head and legs visible.

Project Diagram

Tip:

Uncarded, undyed wool comes straight from a sheared sheep, so it works perfectly for this sheep's fleece.

Wire Frame

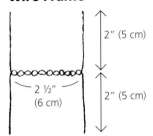

2" (5 cm)

2 ½" (6 cm)

2" (5 cm)

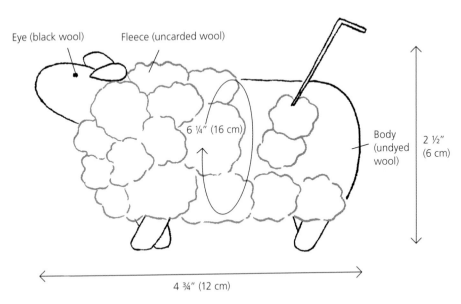

Eye (black wool)

Fleece (uncarded wool)

6 ¼" (16 cm)

Body (undyed wool)

2 ½" (6 cm)

4 ¾" (12 cm)

Cat

Cat

Materials

Wool roving:
- 30 g of brown wool
- 2 g of beige wool
- 2 g of dark brown wool
- Small amount of light pink wool
- Small amount of black wool

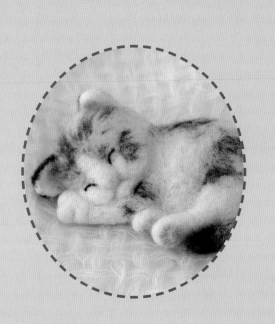

Instructions

Refer to pages 10–15 for a step-by-step photo reference of general felting and assembly techniques.

1. Body: Roll a tuft of undyed wool into a cylinder. Felt to shape the body.

2. Head and Ears: Roll a tuft of undyed wool into a ball and felt into shape. Add wool to the nose and cheeks, then felt into a rounded shape. For the ears, felt small tufts of undyed wool to the head, concentrating the felting at the center to create a curved shape. Join the head and body, **as shown on page 12**.

3. Back Legs: Roll a small tuft of undyed wool into a thin cylinder. Felt one end of the leg, rounding slightly to create a foot, but leave the fibers loose at the other end. Wrap a bit of undyed wool around the top of the leg and felt to attach. Attach the back leg by felting the loose fibers to the body (**refer to page 11**). To create the other back leg, roll a small tuft of undyed wool into a ball and felt to attach to both the back leg and body.

4. Front Legs: Roll a small tuft of undyed wool into a thin cylinder. Felt one end, rounding slightly to create two feet, but leave the fibers loose at the other end. Attach by felting the loose fibers to both the body and head (**refer to page 11**).

5. Tail: Roll a small tuft of undyed wool into a curved cylinder. Felt one end of the tail, leaving the fibers loose at the other end. Felt to attach the loose fibers of the tail to both the body and back leg (**refer to page 13**).

6. Fur: Insert tufts of beige and dark brown wool all over the cat, **as shown in the diagram on the opposite page**, then felt to attach.

7. Nose and Mouth: Roll a tiny ball of light pink wool between your fingertips and felt into a triangular shape. Felt to attach the nose to the head. Use your needle to make an indentation for the mouth.

8. Pads: Roll seven tiny balls and one small ball of light pink wool between your fingertips. Felt to attach four tiny balls and the small ball to one back leg. Felt to attach the remaining three tiny balls to the other back leg.

9. Eyes: Felt two thinly curved strips of black wool to the head.

Tip:
Add wool to give the nose and cheeks a rounded shape.

Project Diagram

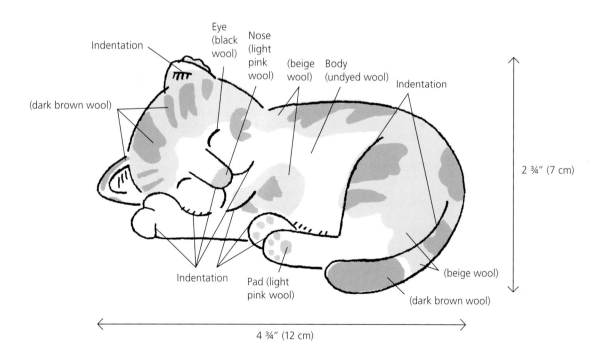

Indentation

Eye (black wool)

Nose (light pink wool)

(beige wool)

Body (undyed wool)

Indentation

(dark brown wool)

2 ¾" (7 cm)

Indentation

Pad (light pink wool)

(beige wool)

(dark brown wool)

4 ¾" (12 cm)

Donkey

Donkey

Materials

Wool roving:
- 15 g of undyed wool
- 3 g of beige wool
- 2 g of dark brown wool
- Small amount of black wool

Wire:
- Two 9 ¾" (25 cm) long pieces of floral wire

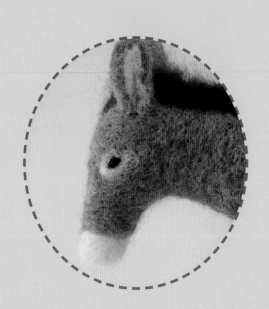

Instructions

Refer to pages 10–15 for a step-by-step photo reference of general felting and assembly techniques.

1. Body: Make the wire frame, **as shown in the diagram on the opposite page**. Cover the legs with brown wool, then felt to attach (**refer to page 13**). Wrap a tuft of brown wool around the center of the wire frame. Felt to shape the body until it is 5 ¼" (13 cm) around the middle.

2. Neck: Roll a tuft of brown wool into a short, thick cylinder. Felt to shape the neck, leaving the fibers loose at both ends. Felt to attach one end of the neck to the body.

3. Head: Roll a tuft of brown wool into a cone and felt into shape. Join the head and neck, **as shown on page 12**.

4. Ears: Roll small tufts of brown wool into two short cylinders. Felt to shape the ears, leaving the fibers loose at one end. Layer a bit of beige wool on top of each ear and felt, concentrating the felting at the center to create a curved shape. Attach ears by felting the loose fibers to the head (**refer to page 12**).

5. Fur: Felt beige wool to the nose tip, legs, and underside of the body. To create eye patches, insert a small tuft of beige wool into each side of the head, then felt to attach.

6. Tail: Make the tail, **as shown on page 73**, using brown wool for the tail and dark brown wool for the tail tip.

7. Hooves: Felt a bit of dark brown wool to the bottom of each leg.

8. Mane: Insert long strips of dark brown wool along the center of the head and neck, **as shown on page 15**.

9. Eyes: Insert small tufts of black wool into the eye patches, then felt into an almond shape.

Project Diagram

Tip:
To give the donkey his signature look, position the head so it is facing down and make the eyes almond-shaped.

Wire Frame

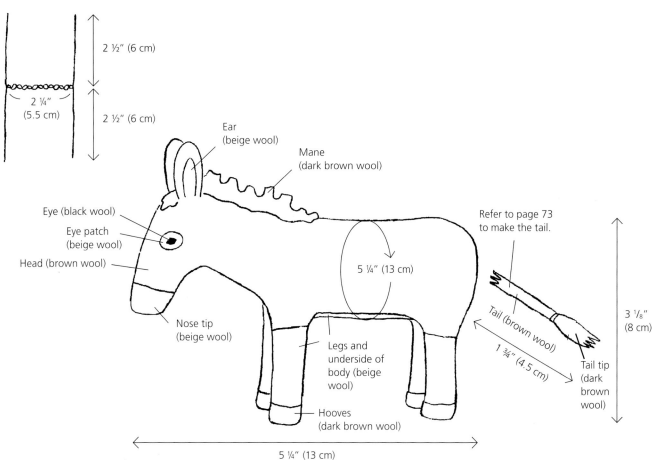

2 ½" (6 cm)

2 ¼" (5.5 cm)

2 ½" (6 cm)

Ear (beige wool)

Mane (dark brown wool)

Eye (black wool)

Eye patch (beige wool)

Head (brown wool)

Nose tip (beige wool)

Refer to page 73 to make the tail.

5 ¼" (13 cm)

Tail (brown wool)

Tail tip (dark brown wool)

3 ⅛" (8 cm)

1 ¾" (4.5 cm)

Legs and underside of body (beige wool)

Hooves (dark brown wool)

5 ¼" (13 cm)

White Tiger

White Tiger

Materials

Wool roving:
- 30 g of undyed wool
- 3 g of black wool
- Small amount of gray wool

Eyes:
- Two 6 mm blue and black eyes

Refer to pages 10–15 for a step-by-step photo reference of general felting and assembly techniques.

1. Body: Roll a tuft of undyed wool into a cylinder. Felt to shape the body until it is 4 ¾" (12 cm) around the middle.

2. Head and Ears: Roll a tuft of undyed wool into a ball and felt into shape. For the ears, felt small tufts of undyed wool to the head, concentrating your felting at the center to create a curved shape. Join the head and body, **as shown on page 12.**

3. Front Legs: Roll small tufts of undyed wool into two thick cylinders. Felt one end of each leg, rounding slightly to create a foot, but leave the fibers loose at the other end. Attach the front legs by felting the loose fibers to the body (**refer to page 11**).

4. Back Legs: Roll small tufts of undyed wool into two cylinders. Felt one end of each leg, rounding slightly to create a foot, but leave the fibers loose at the other end. Wrap a bit of undyed wool around the top of each leg and felt to attach. Attach the back legs by felting the loose fibers to the body (**refer to page 11**).

5. Tail: Roll a small tuft of undyed wool into a curved cylinder. Felt one end of the tail, leaving the fibers loose at the other end. Felt to attach the loose fibers of the tail to the body (**refer to page 13**).

6. Snout: Roll a small tuft of undyed wool into a short cylinder. Felt to attach the snout to the head.

7. Cheeks: Roll two balls of undyed wool between your fingertips. Felt to attach the cheeks to the head and snout.

8. Stripes: Insert thin strips of black wool all over the tiger, **as shown in the diagram on the opposite page,** then felt to attach. Felt black wool to the back of the ears and the tail tip.

9. Nose: Roll a tiny ball of gray wool between your fingertips and felt into a triangular shape. Felt to attach the nose to the snout.

10. Mouth: Felt two thin strips of gray wool to the head, directly beneath the nose. Use your needle to make an indentation.

11. Fur: Insert tufts of undyed wool all over to give the tiger a furry appearance.

12. Eyes: Sew the blue and black eyes to the head (**refer to page 15**).

refer to page 15

Tip:
When making the face, give the nose and cheeks their characteristic feline shape.

Project Diagram

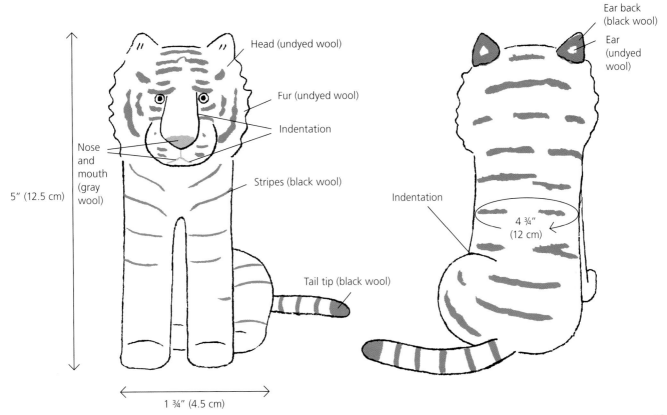

Head (undyed wool)

Fur (undyed wool)

Indentation

Nose and mouth (gray wool)

Stripes (black wool)

5" (12.5 cm)

Tail tip (black wool)

1 ¾" (4.5 cm)

Ear back (black wool)

Ear (undyed wool)

Indentation

4 ¾" (12 cm)

Ducks

Ducks

Materials

ADULT DUCK
Wool roving:
- 20 g of undyed wool
- 2 g of bright yellow wool
- 2 g of orange wool
- 5 g of green wool

Wire:
- One 9 ¾" (25 cm) long piece of floral wire

Eyes:
- Two 4 mm diameter black eyes

Instructions

Refer to pages 10–15 for a step-by-step photo reference of general felting and assembly techniques.

ADULT DUCK

1. Body: Roll a tuft of undyed wool into a semi-circle. Felt to shape the body until it is 8 ½" (21.5 cm) around the middle.

2. Neck: Roll a tuft of undyed wool into a short, thick cylinder. Felt to shape the neck, leaving the fibers loose at both ends. Felt to attach one end of the neck to the body.

3. Head: Roll a tuft of undyed wool into a cone and felt into shape. Join the head and neck, **as shown on page 12**.

4. Wings: Roll tufts of undyed wool into two flat semi-circles. Felt to shape each wing until it is 3 ⅛" (8 cm) around the middle. Felt to attach a wing to each side of the body.

5. Tail: Roll a small tuft of undyed wool into a triangle. Felt one end of the tail, leaving the fibers loose at the other end. Felt to attach the loose fibers of the tail to the body (**refer to page 13**).

6. Beak: Roll a small tuft of bright yellow wool into a cylinder. Felt one end of the beak, flattening slightly, but leave the fibers loose at the other end. Felt to attach the loose fibers of the beak to the head (**refer to page 11**).

7. Legs and Feet: Make the wire frame, **as shown in the diagram on the opposite page**. Felt undyed wool to the legs and orange wool to the feet. Align the legs with the bottom of the body, cover with undyed wool, and felt to attach.

8. Grass: Roll a tuft of green wool into a rectangle and felt into shape. Position the grass behind the legs and felt to attach to the body, legs, and feet. The grass will act as a base to help the duck stand upright.

9. Eyes: Sew a black eye on each side of the head (**refer to page 15**).

Continued on page 48

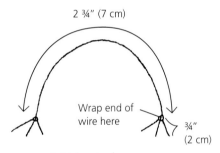

Tip:

Make the body large in proportion to the head. Be careful not to make the neck too long.

Project Diagram

ADULT DUCK

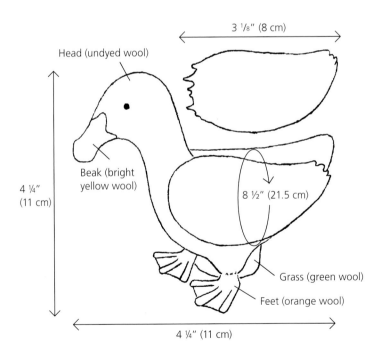

Head (undyed wool)

3 ⅛" (8 cm)

Beak (bright yellow wool)

4 ¼" (11 cm)

8 ½" (21.5 cm)

Grass (green wool)

Feet (orange wool)

4 ¼" (11 cm)

Legs and Feet

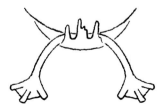

2 ¾" (7 cm)

Wrap end of wire here

¾" (2 cm)

1. Make wire frame and cover with wool.

2. Align legs with body, cover with wool, and felt to attach.

Ducks

Materials (for one baby duck)

BABY DUCK
Wool roving:
- 5 g of light yellow wool
- 2 g of bright yellow wool

Eyes:
- Two 4 mm diameter black eyes

Instructions

Refer to pages 10–15 for a step-by-step photo reference of general felting and assembly techniques.

BABY DUCK

1. Body: Roll a small tuft of light yellow wool into a cone. Felt to shape the body until it is 2 ½" (6 cm) long and 3 ⅛" (8 cm) around the middle.

2. Head: Roll a small tuft of light yellow wool into a ball. Join the head and body, **as shown on page 12**.

3. Beak: Roll a small tuft of bright yellow wool into a cylinder. Felt one end of the beak, flattening slightly, but leave the fibers loose at the other end. Felt to attach the loose fibers of the beak to the head (**refer to page 11**). For an open beak, use scissors to cut a slit, **as shown in the diagram below**.

4. Eyes: Sew a black eye on each side of the head (**refer to page 15**).

BABY DUCK

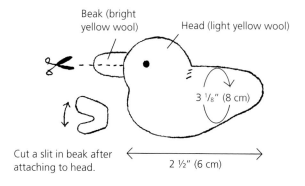

Beak (bright yellow wool)

Head (light yellow wool)

3 ⅛" (8 cm)

Cut a slit in beak after attaching to head.

2 ½" (6 cm)

Pig

Pig

Materials

Wool roving:
- Mixed wool #1: 15 g of ivory wool + 10 g of light pink wool
- Mixed wool #2: Small amount of ivory wool + small amount of dark pink wool (mixed at a 1:1 ratio)

Eyes:
- Two 4 mm diameter black eyes

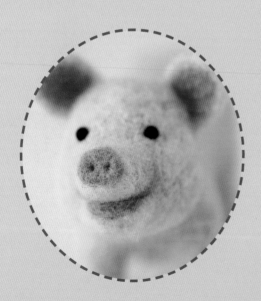

Refer to pages 10–15 for a step-by-step photo reference for felting and assembling the pig.

1. Prepare Wool: Mix the ivory wool with the light pink wool to form mixed wool #1 and the ivory wool with the dark pink wool to form mixed wool #2, **as shown on page 9**.

2. Body: Roll a tuft of mixed wool #1 into a cylinder. Felt to shape the body. Add wool to the pig's rear end and felt into a rounded shape.

3. Legs: Roll small tufts of mixed wool #1 into four cylinders. Felt one end of each leg, rounding slightly to create a foot, but leave the fibers loose at the other end. Attach the legs by felting to loose fibers to the body (**refer to page 11**).

4. Head: Roll a tuft of mixed wool #1 into a ball and felt into shape. For the nose and mouth, roll tiny balls of mixed wool #1 between your fingertips. Felt into shape, leaving the fibers loose at one end. Attach the nose and mouth by felting the loose fibers to the head (**refer to page 11**). Join the head and body, **as shown on page 12**.

5. Ears: Layer small pieces of mixed wool #1 on top of each other and felt both sides, folding the edges in to form triangles. Leave the fibers loose at one end of each ear. Layer a bit of mixed wool #2 on top of each ear and felt, concentrating the felting at the center to create a curved shape. Attach ears by felting the loose fibers to the head (**refer to page 12**).

6. Nose and Mouth: Insert bits of mixed wool #2 into the nose and mouth, then felt to attach. For the nose, use your needle to make two small holes for the nostrils (**refer to page 12**).

7. Tail: Roll a tiny cylinder of mixed wool #2 between your fingertips. Felt one end, leaving the fibers loose at the other end. Attach the tail by felting the loose fibers to the body (**refer to page 13**). Add a small tuft of mixed wool #1, then felt to hide the attachment (**refer to page 14**). Curl the tail using your finger, then felt in place (**refer to page 13**).

8. Eyes: Sew black eyes to the head (**refer to page 15**).

Project Diagram

Tip:

When making the body, add a bit more wool to give the pig's rear end a cute, rounded shape.

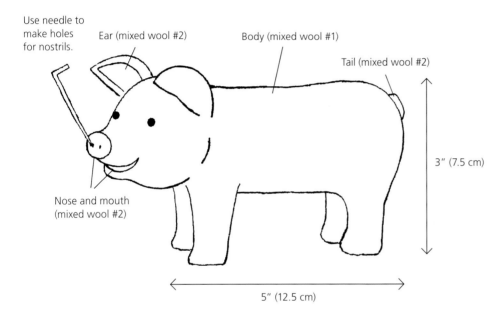

Use needle to make holes for nostrils.

Ear (mixed wool #2)

Body (mixed wool #1)

Tail (mixed wool #2)

Nose and mouth (mixed wool #2)

3" (7.5 cm)

5" (12.5 cm)

Tail

1. Make the tail and attach to the body.
2. Curl the tail and felt in place.

Hippopotamus

Hippopotamus

Materials

Wool roving:
- 40 g of gray wool
- Small amount of light pink wool
- Small amount of undyed wool

Eyes:
- Two 4 mm diameter black eyes

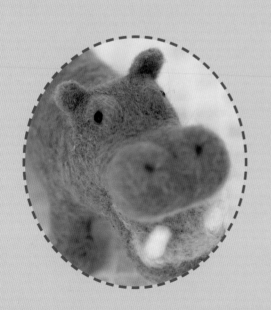

Instructions

Refer to pages 10–15 for a step-by-step photo reference of general felting and assembly techniques.

1. Body: Roll a tuft of gray wool into a cylinder. Felt to shape the body until it is 7″ (18 cm) around the middle.

2. Legs: Roll small tufts of gray wool into four short cylinders. Felt one end of each leg, rounding slightly to create a foot, but leave the fibers loose at the other end. Attach the legs by felting the loose fibers to the body (**refer to page 11**).

3. Tail: Roll a small tuft of gray wool into a triangle. Felt one end of the tail, leaving the fibers loose at the other end. Felt to attach the loose fibers of the tail to the body (**refer to page 13**).

4. Head and Ears: Roll a tuft of gray wool into a rectangle and felt into shape. For the ears, felt small tufts of gray wool to the head, concentrating the felting at the center to create a curved shape. For the eyelids, roll two tiny balls of gray felt between your fingertips. Felt to attach to the head, directly beneath the ears. Join the head and body, **as shown on page 12**.

5. Nose: Roll a small tuft of gray wool into a thin rectangle. Felt one end of the nose, leaving the fibers loose at the other end. Roll two tiny balls of gray felt between your fingers and felt to the tip of the nose. Use your needle to make two small holes for nostrils. Attach nose by felting the loose fibers to the head (**refer to page 11**).

6. Mouth: Roll a small tuft of gray wool into a rectangle. Felt one end of the mouth, leaving the fibers loose at the other end. Attach mouth by felting the loose fibers to the head (**refer to page 11**). Insert a bit of light pink wool into the mouth, then felt to attach (**refer to page 12**).

7. Tusks: Roll two tiny cylinders of undyed wool between your fingertips and felt into shape. Felt to attach the tusks to the inside of the mouth.

8. Eyes: Sew black eyes to the eyelids on the head (**refer to page 15**).

refer to page 15

Tip:

To give the hippopotamus his signature look, make a large, open mouth.

Project Diagram

Nose and Mouth

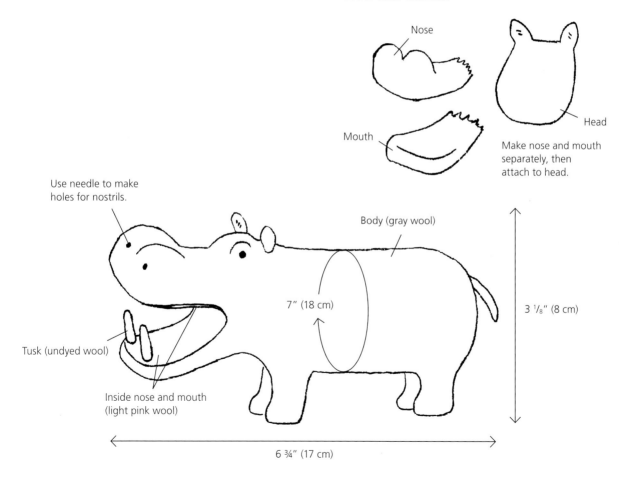

Nose

Mouth

Head

Make nose and mouth separately, then attach to head.

Use needle to make holes for nostrils.

Body (gray wool)

7" (18 cm)

3 1/8" (8 cm)

Tusk (undyed wool)

Inside nose and mouth (light pink wool)

6 ¾" (17 cm)

Chipmunk

Chipmunk

Materials

Wool roving:
- 10 g of undyed wool
- 4 g of brown wool
- 1 g of ivory wool

Eyes:
- Two 6 mm diameter black eyes

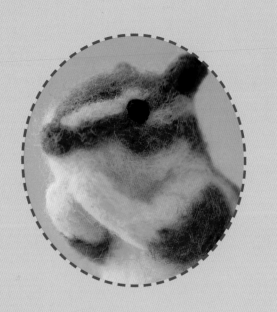

Instructions

Refer to pages 10–15 for a step-by-step photo reference of general felting and assembly techniques.

1. Body: Roll a tuft of undyed wool into an egg. Felt to shape the body until it is 5 ¼" (13.5 cm) around the middle. Add wool to the lower body to give it a rounded shape.

2. Head and Ears: Roll a tuft of undyed wool into a cone and felt into shape. For the ears, felt small tufts of brown wool to the head, concentrating the felting at the center to create a curved shape. Join the head and body, **as shown on page 12**.

3. Arms: Roll small tufts of undyed wool into two thin cylinders. Felt one end of each arm, leaving the fibers loose at the other end. Attach the arms by felting the loose fibers to the body (**refer to page 11**). Add wool to each attachment and felt into a rounded shape. Bend the arms and felt in place.

4. Legs: To create the haunches, felt small tufts of brown wool into two circles and attach to the body. For the legs, roll small tufts of brown wool into two short cylinders. Felt one end of each leg, leaving the fibers loose at the other end. Attach the legs by felting the loose fibers to the body (**refer to page 11**).

5. Tail: Roll a small tuft of brown wool into a 2 ¼" (6 cm) long cylinder Lightly felt one end of the tail, leaving the fibers loose at the other end. Attach the tail by felting the loose fibers to the body (**refer to page 13**). Insert tufts of brown wool into the tail to give it a bushy appearance.

6. Eyes: Sew a black eye on each side of the head (**refer to page 15**).

7. Fur: Insert thin strips of brown and ivory wool all over the chipmunk, **as shown in the diagram on the opposite page**, then felt to attach.

8. Nose: Roll a tiny ball of brown wool between your fingertips. Felt to attach the nose to the head.

9. Finish: Felt the tips of the arms to the chipmunk's mouth.

Tip:

Make sure to sew the eyes to the head before adding the fur.

Project Diagram

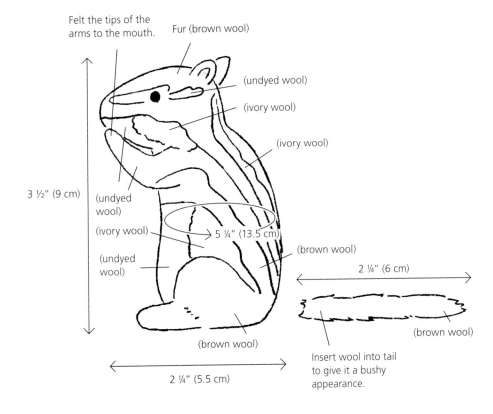

Create curved shape when felting the ears.

Indentation

1 ½" (4 cm)

1 ¼" (3 cm)

Felt the tips of the arms to the mouth.

Fur (brown wool)

(undyed wool)

(ivory wool)

(ivory wool)

3 ½" (9 cm)

(undyed wool)

(ivory wool)

5 ¼" (13.5 cm)

(undyed wool)

(brown wool)

2 ¼" (6 cm)

(brown wool)

(brown wool)

2 ¼" (5.5 cm)

Insert wool into tail to give it a bushy appearance.

Brown Bear

Brown Bear

Materials

Wool roving:
- 35 g of brown wool
- Small amount of black wool

Eyes:
- Two 4 mm diameter black eyes

Instructions

Refer to pages 10–15 for a step-by-step photo reference of general felting and assembly techniques.

1. Body: Roll a tuft of brown wool into a cylinder. Felt to shape the body until it is 6" (15 cm) around the middle. Add wool to the upper back to give it a rounded shape.

2. Head and Ears: Roll a tuft of brown wool into a cone and felt into shape. Add wool to the head to make a snout. For the ears, felt small tufts of brown wool to the head, concentrating the felting at the center to create a curved shape. Join the head and body, **as shown on page 12**.

3. Legs: Roll small tufts of brown wool into four cylinders. Felt one end of each leg, rounding slightly to create a foot, but leave the fibers loose at the other end. Attach the legs by felting the loose fibers to the body (**refer to page 11**).

4. Nose and Mouth: Roll a tiny ball of black wool between your fingertips. Felt to attach the nose to the head. Use your needle to make an indentation for the mouth.

5. Eyes: Sew black eyes to the head (**refer to page 15**).

Project Diagram

Tip:

Project instructions are not included for the bear cub. Simply make a smaller version of the adult and position the cub so it's sitting down.

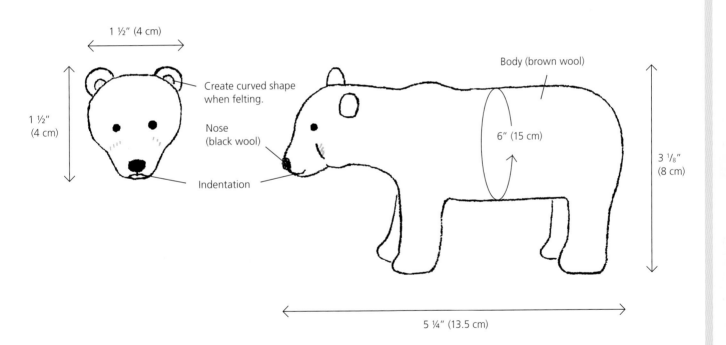

1 ½" (4 cm)

1 ½" (4 cm)

Create curved shape when felting.

Nose (black wool)

Indentation

Body (brown wool)

6" (15 cm)

3 ⅛" (8 cm)

5 ¼" (13.5 cm)

Giant Panda

Giant Panda

Materials

Wool roving:
- 30 g of undyed wool
- 10 g of black wool

Eyes:
- Two 4 mm diameter black eyes

Instructions

Refer to pages 10–15 for a step-by-step photo reference of general felting and assembly techniques.

1. Body: Roll a tuft of undyed wool into an egg. Felt to shape the body until it is 7" (18 cm) around the middle.

2. Head: Roll a tuft of undyed wool into a ball and felt into shape. For the snout, roll a small tuft of undyed wool into a ball, then felt to attach to the head. Join the head and body, **as shown on page 12**.

3. Ears: Felt small tufts of black wool into circles, concentrating the felting at the center to create a curved shape. Felt to attach the ears to the head, then cover the attachment with undyed wool, **as shown on page 14**.

4. Arms: Roll small tufts of black wool into two thick cylinders. Felt one end of each arm, leaving the fibers loose at the other end. Attach the arms by felting the loose fibers to the body (**refer to page 11**). Bend the arms and felt in place. Felt black wool to the upper back.

5. Legs: Roll small tufts of black wool into two thick cylinders. Felt one end of each leg, rounding slightly to create a foot, but leave the fibers loose at the other end. Attach the legs by felting the loose fibers to the body (**refer to page 11**).

6. Eyes: To create eye patches, insert small tufts of black wool into the head, then felt to attach. Sew black eyes to the eye patches (**refer to page 15**).

7. Nose and Mouth: Roll a tiny ball of black wool between your fingertips. Felt to attach the nose to the snout. Use your needle to make an indentation for the mouth.

Tip:

Make the body, arms, and legs thick to capture the panda's plump look.

Project Diagram

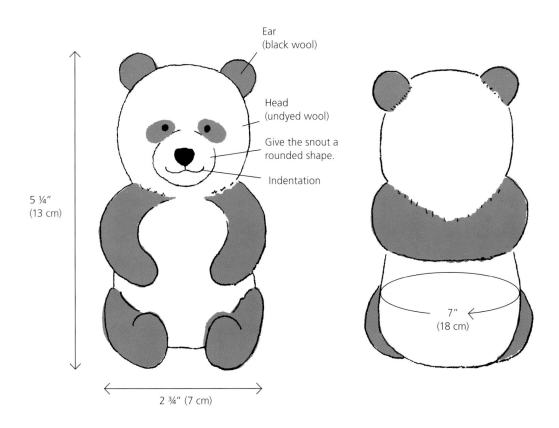

Ear
(black wool)

Head
(undyed wool)

Give the snout a
rounded shape.

Indentation

5 ¼"
(13 cm)

2 ¾" (7 cm)

7"
(18 cm)

Elephant

Elephant

Materials

Wool roving:
- 60 g of gray wool
- 3 g of undyed wool

Eyes:
- Two 6 mm diameter black eyes

Instructions

Refer to pages 10–15 for a step-by-step photo reference of general felting and assembly techniques.

1. Body: Roll a tuft of gray wool into a cylinder. Felt to shape the body until it is 7 ½" (19 cm) around the middle.

2. Head: Roll a tuft of gray wool into a ball and felt into shape. Join the head and body, **as shown on page 12**.

3. Legs: Roll small tufts of gray wool into four thick cylinders. Felt one end of each leg, rounding slightly to create a foot, but leave the fibers loose at the other end. Attach the legs by felting the loose fibers to the body (**refer to page 11**).

4. Ears: Felt small tufts of gray wool into two bean shapes. Felt to attach the ears to the head.

5. Trunk: Roll a small tuft of gray wool into a curved cylinder. Felt one end of the trunk, leaving the fibers loose at the other end. Attach the trunk by felting the loose fibers to the head.

6. Mouth: Felt a tiny tuft of gray wool to the head, directly below the trunk.

7. Tail: Roll a small tuft of gray wool into a cylinder and felt, leaving the fibers loose at both ends. Felt to attach a tuft of gray wool to the tail tip. Attach the tail by felting the loose fibers to the body (**refer to page 13**).

8. Tusks: Roll small tufts of undyed wool into two 1 ¾" (4.5 cm) long curved cylinders. Felt one end of each tusk, creating a point, but leave the fibers loose at the other end. Attach the tusks by felting the loose fibers to the head.

9. Hooves: Felt four tiny circles of undyed wool to each front leg and three tiny circles of undyed wool to each back leg.

10. Eyes: Sew a black eye to each side of the head (**refer to page 15**).

When shaping the trunk,
make it thicker at the base
and thinner at the tip.

Project Diagram

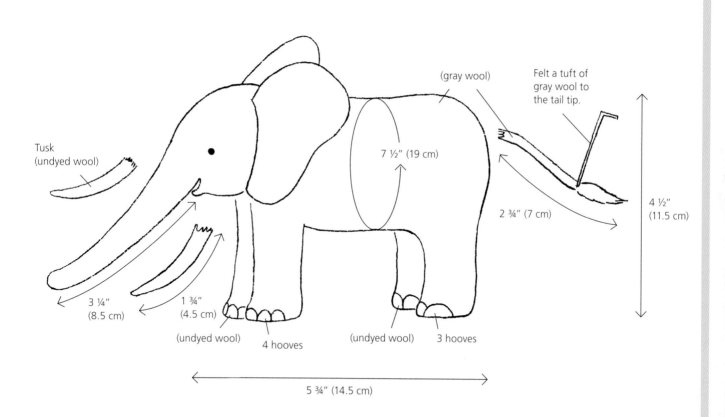

(gray wool)

Felt a tuft of
gray wool to
the tail tip.

Tusk
(undyed wool)

7 ½" (19 cm)

2 ¾" (7 cm)

4 ½"
(11.5 cm)

3 ¼"
(8.5 cm)

1 ¾"
(4.5 cm)

(undyed wool)

4 hooves

(undyed wool)

3 hooves

5 ¾" (14.5 cm)

Owl

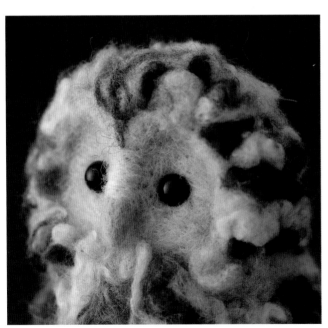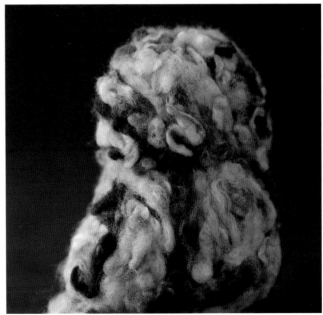

Owl

Materials

Wool roving:
- 20 g of beige wool
- Small amount of bright yellow wool

Uncarded wool:
- 6 g of mixed color uncarded wool

Eyes:
- Two 7 mm diameter black eyes

Instructions

Refer to pages 10–15 for a step-by-step photo reference of general felting and assembly techniques.

1. Body: Roll a tuft of beige wool into an egg. Felt to shape the body until it is 8 ¼" (21 cm) around the middle.

2. Head: Roll a tuft of beige wool into a ball and felt into shape. Join the head and body, **as shown on page 12**.

3. Tail: Roll a small tuft of beige wool into a triangle. Felt one end of the tail, leaving the fibers loose at the other end. Attach the tail by felting the loose fibers to the body (**refer to page 13**).

4. Beak: Roll a small tuft of bright yellow wool into a cylinder. Felt one end of the beak, creating a point, but leave the fibers loose at the other end. Wrap a bit of beige wool around the top of the beak and felt to attach. Felt to attach the beak to the head.

5. Feathers: Insert tufts of mixed color uncarded wool into the head and body and felt to attach, leaving the face and tail visible.

6. Eyes: Sew black eyes to the head (**refer to page 15**).

Tip:

When inserting the uncarded wool for the owl's feathers, pay attention to the color of the wool and the pattern it creates.

Project Diagram

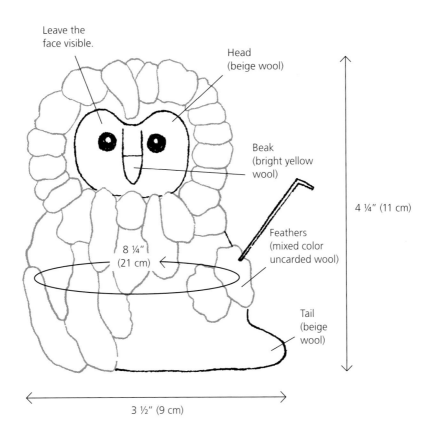

Leave the face visible.

Head (beige wool)

Beak (bright yellow wool)

Feathers (mixed color uncarded wool)

Tail (beige wool)

4 ¼" (11 cm)

8 ¼" (21 cm)

3 ½" (9 cm)

Paddybird

Paddybird

Materials

Wool roving:
- 12 g of undyed wool
- 2 g of light pink wool
- Small amount of maroon wool

Wire:
- One 9 ¾" (25 cm) long piece of floral wire

Eyes:
- Two 4 mm diameter black eyes

Instructions

Refer to pages 10–15 for a step-by-step photo reference of general felting and assembly techniques.

1. Body: Roll a tuft of undyed wool into a thin semi-circle. Felt to shape the body until it is 5 ½" (14 cm) around the middle.

2. Head: Roll a tuft of beige wool into a ball and felt into shape. Join the head and body, **as shown on page 12**.

3. Wings: Roll tufts of undyed wool into two flat semi-circles. Felt to shape each wing until it is 2 ¾" (7 cm) long. Felt to attach a wing to each side of the body.

4. Tail: Roll a small tuft of undyed wool into a rectangle. Felt one end of the tail, leaving the fibers loose at the other end. Attach the tail by felting the loose fibers to the body (**refer to page 13**). Use your needle to make an indentation down the center of the tail.

5. Beak: Roll a small tuft of maroon wool into a triangle. Felt one end of the beak, creating a point, but leave the fibers loose at the other end. Attach the beak by felting the loose fibers to the head (**refer to page 11**). Felt a bit of undyed wool to the beak tip. Use your needle to make an indentation down the center of the beak.

6. Legs and Feet: Make the wire frame, **as shown in the diagram on the opposite page**. Felt light pink wool to the legs and feet. Align the legs with the bottom of the body, cover with undyed wool, and felt to attach.

7. Eyes: Insert small tufts of maroon wool into the head, then felt to attach. Sew black eyes to the maroon felt (**refer to page 15**).

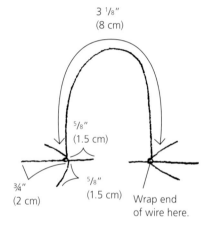

Tip:

Make the beak large in proportion to the paddybird's head.

Project Diagram

Legs and Feet

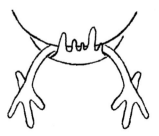

3 ¹/₈"
(8 cm)

⁵/₈"
(1.5 cm)

¾"
(2 cm)

⁵/₈"
(1.5 cm)

Wrap end
of wire here.

1. Make wire frame
and cover with wool.

2. Align legs with body, cover
with wool, and felt to attach.

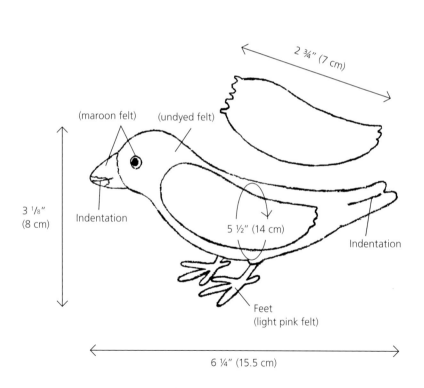

2 ¾" (7 cm)

(maroon felt)

(undyed felt)

Indentation

3 ¹/₈"
(8 cm)

5 ½" (14 cm)

Indentation

Feet
(light pink felt)

6 ¼" (15.5 cm)

Goat

Goat

Materials

Wool roving:
- 17 g of undyed wool
- Small amount of light pink wool
- Small amount of black wool

Wire:
- Two 9 ¾" (25 cm) long pieces of floral wire

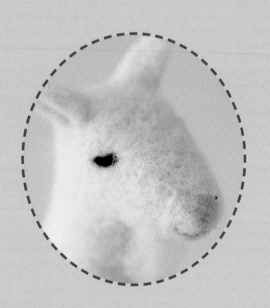

Instructions

Refer to pages 10–15 for a step-by-step photo reference of general felting and assembly techniques.

1. Body: Make the wire frame, **as shown in the diagram on the opposite page**. Cover the legs with undyed wool, then felt to attach (**refer to page 13**). Wrap a tuft of undyed wool around the center of the wire frame. Felt to shape the body until it is 5 ¼" (13.5 cm) around the middle.

2. Neck: Roll a tuft of undyed wool into a short, thick cylinder. Felt to shape the neck, leaving the fibers loose at both ends. Felt to attach one end of the neck to the body.

3. Head: Roll a tuft of undyed wool into a cone and felt into shape. Join the head and neck, **as shown on page 12**.

4. Tail: Make the tail, **as shown on page 73**, using undyed wool.

5. Ears: Roll small tufts of undyed wool into two short cylinders. Felt to shape the ears, leaving the fibers loose at one end. Layer a bit of light pink wool on top of each ear and felt, concentrating the felting at the center to create a curved shape. Attach ears by felting the loose fibers to the head (**refer to page 12**).

6. Nose and Mouth: Roll a tiny ball of light pink wool between your fingertips. Felt to attach the nose to the head. For the mouth, felt two strips of light pink wool to the head, directly beneath the nose.

7. Beard: Insert a tuft of undyed wool into the chin and felt to attach.

8. Eyes: Felt two thin strips of black wool to the head.

Project Diagram

Tip:

Goats have surprisingly long necks, so continue adding wool to the neck until you achieve the correct proportion.

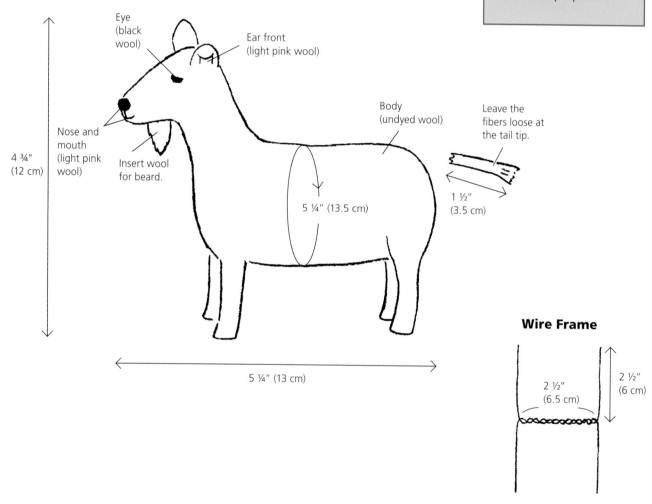

Eye (black wool)

Ear front (light pink wool)

Nose and mouth (light pink wool)

Insert wool for beard.

Body (undyed wool)

Leave the fibers loose at the tail tip.

4 ¾" (12 cm)

5 ¼" (13.5 cm)

1 ½" (3.5 cm)

5 ¼" (13 cm)

Wire Frame

2 ½" (6.5 cm)

2 ½" (6 cm)

Green Frog

Green Frog

Materials

Wool roving:
- 10 g of light green wool
- Small amount of white wool
- Small amount of black wool

Refer to pages 10–15 for a step-by-step photo reference of general felting and assembly techniques.

1. Body: Roll a tufts of light green wool into an egg. Felt to shape the body.

2. Head: Roll a tuft of light green wool into a cone and felt into shape. Roll two tiny balls of light green felt between your fingertips. Felt to attach to the head. Join the head and body, **as shown on page 12**.

3. Back Legs: For the feet, roll small tufts of light green wool into two flat circles. Felt to shape the feet, using your needle to create indentations for the toes. Roll small tufts of light green wool into two cylinders and felt, leaving the fibers loose at both ends. Felt to attach the feet to the back legs. Attach the back legs by felting the loose fibers to the body (**refer to page 11**). Bend each back leg at the knee and felt to attach the calf to the body. Bend each back leg at the ankle and felt in place.

4. Front Legs: Roll small tufts of light green wool into two cylinders and felt, leaving the fibers loose at both ends. For the feet, roll small tufts of light green wool into two flat circles. Felt to attach the feet to the front legs. Cut three slits into each foot, then felt into shape to create four toes, **as shown in the diagram on the opposite page**. Attach the front legs by felting the loose fibers to the body (**refer to page 11**). Bend the front legs and felt in place.

5. Eyes: Roll tiny tufts of white wool into two flat circles. Insert the circles into the rounded areas of the head, then felt to attach. Felt two thin strips of black wool to the white circles.

Project Diagram

Front Legs

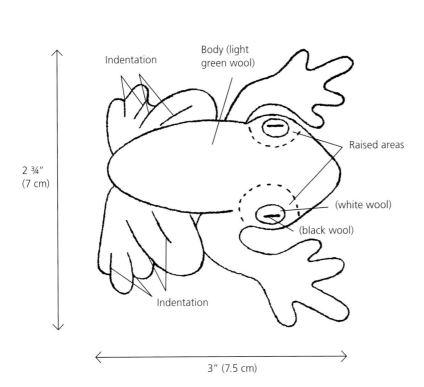

Indentation

Body (light
green wool)

Raised areas

(white wool)

(black wool)

Indentation

2 ¾"
(7 cm)

3" (7.5 cm)

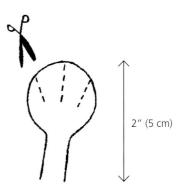

2" (5 cm)

1. Cut three slits
into each foot.

2. Felt to create four toes.

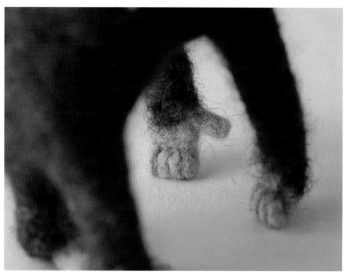

Chimpanzees

Chimpanzees

Materials

ADULT CHIMPANZEE
Wool roving:
- 25 g of light brown wool
- 5 g of black wool
- Small amount of brown wool

Eyes:
- Two 6 mm diameter dark brown eyes

Instructions

Refer to pages 10–15 for a step-by-step photo reference of general felting and assembly techniques.

ADULT CHIMPANZEE

1. Body: Roll a tuft of light brown wool into a cylinder. Felt to shape the body until it is 5 ½" (13 cm) around the middle.

2. Head and Ears: Roll a tuft of light brown wool into an oval and felt into shape. Add wool to the forehead, nose, and mouth areas, then felt into a rounded shape. For the ears, felt small tufts of wool to the head, concentrating the felting at the center to create a curved shape. Join the head and body, **as shown on page 12**.

3. Arms and Legs: Roll small tufts of light brown wool into four thin cylinders. Felt one end of each arm/leg, leaving the fibers loose at the other end (**refer to page 11**). To create hands and feet, fold ends of the arms and legs, then felt into a square. To the hands only, add a small rectangle of light brown wool for fingers and felt to attach. To make the thumbs, roll tiny tufts of light brown wool into four thin cylinders. Felt to attach the thumbs to both the hands and feet. Attach the arms and legs by felting the loose fibers to the body (**refer to page 11**).

4. Fur: Felt black wool to the body, head, arms, and legs, leaving the face, ears, hands, and feet visible.

5. Finger and Toes: Felt thin strips of brown wool to the hands and feet.

6. Face: Felt two tiny balls of brown wool to the nose and a thin strip of brown wool to the mouth. Sew the eyes to the head (**refer to page 15**).

Continued on page 94

Project Diagram

ADULT CHIMPANZEE

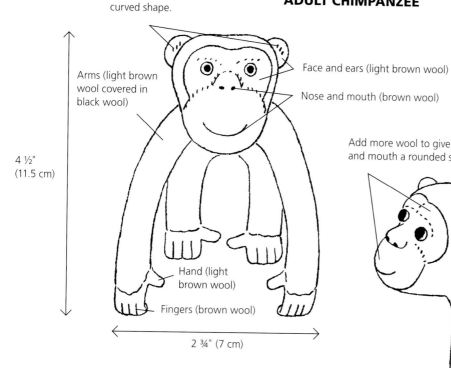

Concentrate felting at center to create curved shape.

Arms (light brown wool covered in black wool)

Face and ears (light brown wool)

Nose and mouth (brown wool)

4 ½" (11.5 cm)

Hand (light brown wool)

Fingers (brown wool)

2 ¾" (7 cm)

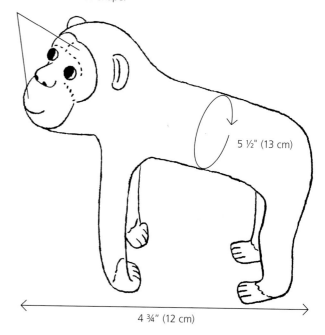

Add more wool to give forehead and mouth a rounded shape.

5 ½" (13 cm)

4 ¾" (12 cm)

Chimpanzees

Materials

BABY CHIMPANZEE
Wool roving:
- 6 g of peach wool
- 2 g of black wool
- Small amount of light brown wool

Eyes:
- Two 4 mm diameter black eyes

Instructions

Refer to pages 10–15 for a step-by-step photo reference of general felting and assembly techniques.

BABY CHIMPANZEE

1. Body, Head, and Ears: Repeat steps 1–2 to make the body, head, and ears, **according to the dimensions on the opposite page**. Use peach wool for the baby's body, head, and ears.

2. Arms and Legs: Roll tufts of peach wool into four thin cylinders. Felt one end of each arm/leg, rounding slightly to create hands/feet, but leave the fibers loose at the other end. Attach the arms/legs by felting the loose fibers to the body (**refer to page 11**). Bend the arms and legs and felt in place.

3. Fur: Felt black wool to the body, head, arms, and legs, leaving the face, ears, hands, and feet visible.

4. Face: Repeat step 6 to make the baby's face, using light brown wool.

5. Finish: Position the baby on the adult's back and felt to attach.

Tip:

Before felting the arms in shape, position the baby on the adult's back to determine the angles at which to bend the baby's arms.

Project Diagram

BABY CHIMPANZEE

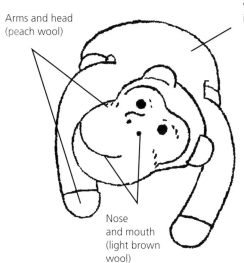

Arms and head (peach wool)

Body (peach wool covered in black wool)

Nose and mouth (light brown wool)

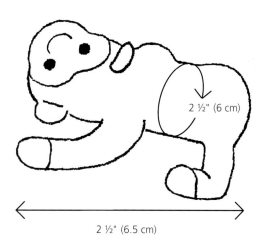

2 ½" (6 cm)

2 ½" (6.5 cm)

Giraffe

Giraffe

Materials

Wool roving:
- 30 g of ivory wool
- 5 g of reddish brown wool
- 2 g of brown wool

Wire:
- Three 9 ¾" (25 cm) long pieces of floral wire

Eyes:
- Two 4 mm diameter black eyes

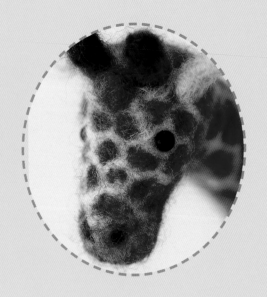

Instructions

Refer to pages 10–15 for a step-by-step photo reference of general felting and assembly techniques.

1. Body: Make the wire frame, **as shown in the diagram on the opposite page**. Cover the legs with ivory wool, then felt to attach (**refer to page 13**). Wrap a tuft of ivory wool around the center of the wire frame. Felt to shape the body until it is 5 ¼" (13 cm) around the middle. Cover the neck with ivory wool, then felt to attach

2. Head and Ears: Roll a tuft of ivory wool into a cone and felt into shape. For the ears, felt small tufts of ivory wool to the head, concentrating the felting at the center to create a curved shape. Join the head and neck, **as shown on page 12**.

3. Horns: Roll two tiny cylinders of reddish brown wool between your fingertips and felt into shape. Felt brown wool to the horn tips. Felt to attach the horns to the head.

4. Bump: Roll a tiny ball of reddish brown wool between your fingertips and felt into shape. Felt to attach the bump to the head, directly beneath the horns.

5. Tail: Make the tail, **as shown on page 73**, using ivory wool for the tail and brown wool for the tail tip.

6. Spots: Insert small tufts of reddish brown wool all over the giraffe, **as shown in the diagram on the opposite page**, then felt to attach.

7. Nose: Felt reddish brown wool to the nose. Insert tiny tufts of brown wool into the nose to create two nostrils.

8. Hooves: Felt a bit of brown wool to the bottom of each leg.

9. Eyes: Sew black eyes to the head (**refer to page 15**).

Project Diagram

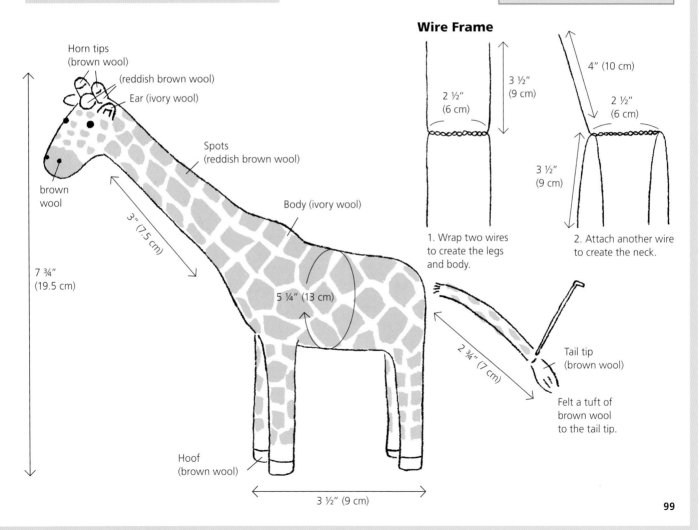

Horn tips
(brown wool)

(reddish brown wool)

Ear (ivory wool)

Spots
(reddish brown wool)

Body (ivory wool)

brown
wool

3" (7.5 cm)

7 ¾"
(19.5 cm)

5 ¼" (13 cm)

Hoof
(brown wool)

3 ½" (9 cm)

Wire Frame

2 ½"
(6 cm)

3 ½"
(9 cm)

1. Wrap two wires to create the legs and body.

4" (10 cm)

2 ½"
(6 cm)

3 ½"
(9 cm)

2. Attach another wire to create the neck.

2 ¾" (7 cm)

Tail tip
(brown wool)

Felt a tuft of
brown wool
to the tail tip.

Lions

Lions

Materials

MALE LION
Wool roving:
- 20 g of ivory wool
- Mixed wool #1: 4 g of light brown wool + 4 g of golden yellow wool
- Mixed wool #2: 1 g of light brown wool + 1 g of golden yellow wool + 1 g of brown wool
- 2 g of brown wool

Wire:
- Two 9 ¾" (25 cm) long pieces of floral wire

Eyes:
- Two 6 mm diameter light brown eyes

Instructions

Refer to pages 10–15 for a step-by-step photo reference of general felting and assembly techniques.

MALE LION

1. Body: Make the wire frame, **as shown in the diagram on the opposite page**. Cover the legs with ivory wool, then felt to attach (**refer to page 13**). Wrap a tufts of ivory wool around the center of the wire frame. Felt to shape the body until it is 4 ¼" (11 cm) around the middle.

2. Neck: Roll a tuft of ivory wool into a short, thick cylinder and felt to shape the neck, leaving the fibers loose at both ends. Felt to attach one end of the neck to the body.

3. Head: Roll a tuft of ivory wool into a cone and felt into shape. Add wool to the nose and felt into a rounded shape. Join the head and neck, **as shown on page 12**.

4. Prepare Wool: Mix the light brown wool with golden yellow wool to form mixed wool #1, **as shown on page 9**.

5. Ears: Felt small tufts of mixed wool #1 to the head, concentrating the felting at the center to create a curved shape.

6. Tail: Make the tail, **as shown on page 73**, using mixed wool #1 for the tail and brown wool for the tail tip.

7. Fur: Felt mixed wool #1 to the lion, leaving only the mouth visible.

8. Nose and Mouth: Roll a tiny ball of brown wool between your fingertips. Felt to attach the nose to the head. For the mouth, felt two thin strips of brown wool to head, directly beneath the nose.

9. Eyes: Sew light brown eyes to the head (**refer to page 15**).

10. Mane: Mix the light brown wool, golden yellow wool, and brown wool to form mixed wool #2, **as shown on page 9**. Insert tufts of mixed wool #2 and brown wool into the head and neck (**refer to page 15**).

Continued on page 104

Project Diagram

Tip:

When making the mane, insert a section of solid brown wool behind the section of mixed wool #2.

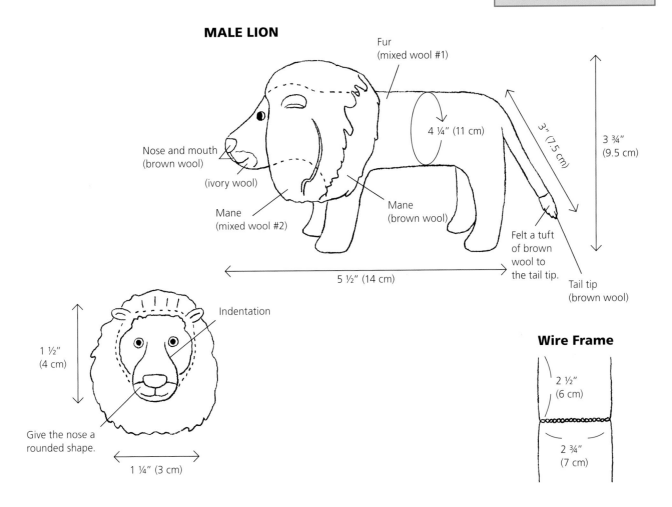

MALE LION

Fur
(mixed wool #1)

Nose and mouth
(brown wool)

(ivory wool)

Mane
(mixed wool #2)

Mane
(brown wool)

4 ¼" (11 cm)

3" (7.5 cm)

3 ¾"
(9.5 cm)

Felt a tuft
of brown
wool to
the tail tip.

Tail tip
(brown wool)

5 ½" (14 cm)

Indentation

1 ½"
(4 cm)

Give the nose a
rounded shape.

1 ¼" (3 cm)

Wire Frame

2 ½"
(6 cm)

2 ¾"
(7 cm)

103

Lions

Materials

FEMALE LION
Wool roving:
- 20 g of ivory wool
- Mixed wool: 4 g of light brown wool + 4 g of golden yellow wool
- 2 g of brown wool

Eyes:
- Two 6 mm diameter light brown eyes

Instructions

Refer to pages 10–15 for a step-by-step photo reference of general felting and assembly techniques.

FEMALE LION

1. Body: Roll a tuft of ivory wool into a cylinder. Felt to shape the body until it is 4 ¼" (11 cm) around the middle.

2. Neck: Roll a tuft of ivory wool into a short, thick cylinder and felt to shape the neck, leaving the fibers loose at both ends. Felt to attach one end of the neck to the body.

3. Head: Roll a tuft of ivory wool into a cone and felt into shape. Add wool to the nose and felt into a rounded shape. Join the head and neck, **as shown on page 12**.

4. Back Legs: Roll a small tuft of ivory wool into a cylinder. Felt one end of the leg, rounding slightly to create a foot, but leave the fibers loose at the other end. Wrap a bit of ivory wool around the top of the leg and felt to attach. Attach the back leg by felting the loose fibers to the body (**refer to page 11**). Bend the leg and felt in place. To create the other back leg, roll a small tuft of ivory wool into a cylinder and felt to attach to both the back leg and body.

5. Front Legs: Roll small tufts of ivory wool into two cylinders. Felt one end of each leg, rounding slightly to create a foot, but the leave the fibers loose at the other end. Use your needle to create indentations in the foot. Attach the front legs by felting the loose fibers to the body (**refer to page 11**).

6. Prepare Wool: Mix the light brown wool with golden yellow wool to form the mixed wool, **as shown on page 9**.

7. Ears: Felt small tufts of the mixed wool to the head, concentrating the felting at the center to create a curved shape.

8. Tail: Make the tail, **as shown on page 73**, using the mixed wool for the tail and brown wool for the tail tip.

9. Fur: Felt the mixed wool to the lion, leaving the mouth, underside, and feet visible.

10. Nose and Mouth: Roll a tiny ball of brown wool between your fingertips. Felt to attach the nose to the head. For the mouth, felt two thin strips of brown wool to head, directly beneath the nose.

11. Eyes: Sew light brown eyes to the head (**refer to page 15**).

Tip:
Project instructions are not included for the lion cubs. Simply make smaller versions of the female lion—just use short cylinders for the lion cubs' legs.

Project Diagram

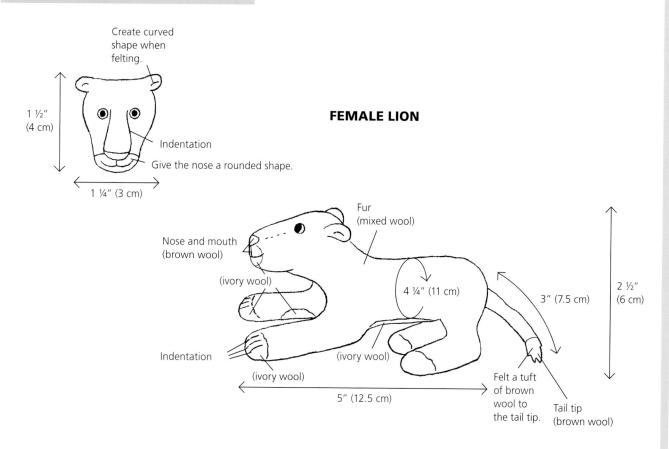

Create curved shape when felting.

1 ½" (4 cm)

Indentation

Give the nose a rounded shape.

1 ¼" (3 cm)

FEMALE LION

Fur (mixed wool)

Nose and mouth (brown wool)

(ivory wool)

4 ¼" (11 cm)

3" (7.5 cm)

2 ½" (6 cm)

Indentation

(ivory wool)

(ivory wool)

Felt a tuft of brown wool to the tail tip.

Tail tip (brown wool)

5" (12.5 cm)

Brussels Griffon

Brussels Griffon

Materials

Wool roving:
- 20 g of ivory wool
- Mixed wool #1: 1 g of reddish brown wool + 1 g of golden yellow wool + 1 g of brown wool
- Mixed wool #2: 2 g of light brown wool + 2 g of golden yellow wool + 2 g of ivory wool
- Small amount of dark brown wool
- Small amount of black wool

Eyes:
- Two 6 mm diameter black eyes

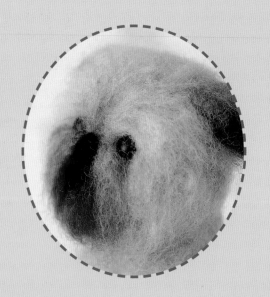

Instructions

Refer to pages 10–15 for a step-by-step photo reference of general felting and assembly techniques.

1. Body: Roll a tuft of ivory wool into a cylinder. Felt to shape the body until it is 5 ¼" (13 cm) around the middle.

2. Head: Roll a tuft of ivory wool into a ball and felt into shape. Join the head and neck, **as shown on page 12**.

3. Back Legs: Roll small tufts of ivory wool into two cylinders. Felt one end of each leg, rounding slightly to create a foot, but leave the fibers loose at the other end. Wrap a bit of ivory wool around the top of each leg and felt to attach. Attach the back legs by felting the loose fibers to the body (**refer to page 11**).

4. Front Legs: Roll small tufts of ivory wool into two cylinders. Felt one end of each leg, rounding slightly to create a foot, but leave the fibers loose at the other end. Attach the front legs by felting the loose fibers to the body (**refer to page 11**).

5. Prepare Wool: Mix the reddish brown wool, golden yellow wool, and brown wool to form mixed wool #1, **as shown on page 9**.

6. Ears: Felt small tufts of mixed wool #1 to the head, concentrating the felting at the center to create a curved shape.

7. Feet: Felt a bit of mixed wool #1 to the bottom of each leg.

8. Nose and Mouth: Form a tiny disc of black wool between your fingertips. Felt to attach the nose to the head. For the mouth, felt two thin strips of black wool to head, directly beneath the nose.

9. Eyes: Sew black eyes to the head (**refer to page 15**).

10. Fur: Mix the light brown wool, golden yellow wool, and ivory wool to form mixed wool #2, **as shown on page 9**. Insert tufts of mixed wool #2 around the nose. Insert tufts of dark brown wool at the ear tips and around the mouth.

11. Tail: Felt a small tuft of mixed wool #2 to the rear end.

Tip:

The small, flat nose is a unique characteristic of the Brussels Griffon breed. When inserting the fur, make the area around the dog's mouth the darkest in color.

Project Diagram

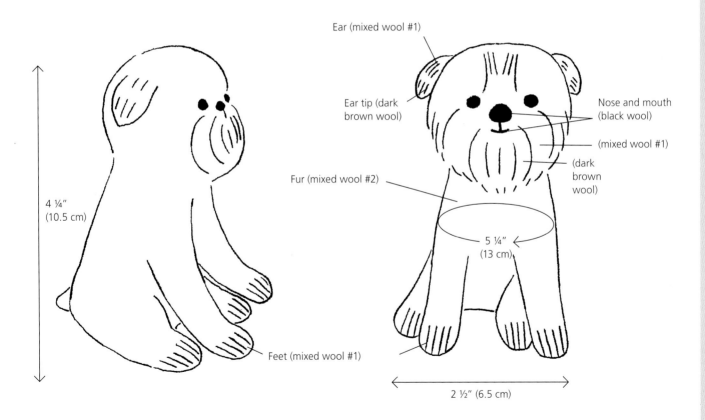

4 ¼" (10.5 cm)

Feet (mixed wool #1)

Ear (mixed wool #1)

Ear tip (dark brown wool)

Nose and mouth (black wool)

(mixed wool #1)

(dark brown wool)

Fur (mixed wool #2)

5 ¼" (13 cm)

2 ½" (6.5 cm)

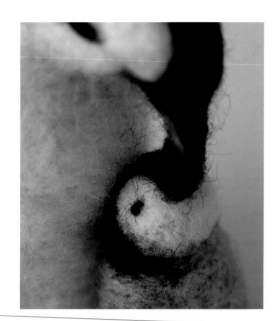

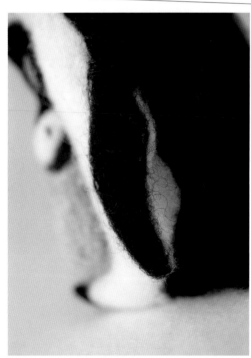

Emperor Penguins

Emperor Penguins

Materials

ADULT PENGUIN
Wool roving:
- 40 g of undyed wool
- 5 g of black wool
- Small amount of bright yellow wool
- Small amount of cream wool
- Small amount of salmon pink wool
- Small amount of charcoal gray wool

Eyes:
- Two 4 mm diameter black eyes

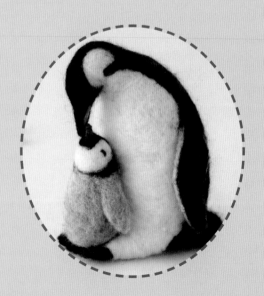

Instructions

Refer to pages 10–15 for a step-by-step photo reference of general felting and assembly techniques.

ADULT PENGUIN

1. Body: Roll a tuft of undyed wool into an egg. Felt to shape the body until it is 9 ½" (24 cm) around the middle. Add wool to the upper body to give it a rounded shape.

2. Head: Roll a tuft of undyed wool into a small egg and felt into shape. Join the head and body, **as shown on page 12**.

3. Flippers: Form tufts of undyed wool into two flat boomerang shapes. Felt to shape each flipper so it is 2 ¾" (7 cm) long. Felt to attach a flipper to each side of the body.

4. Markings: Refer to the diagram on the opposite page to felt black wool to the head, back, and outer flipper, bright yellow wool to the head, and cream wool to the body. Insert small tufts of charcoal gray wool into the back and lightly felt.

5. Beak: Roll a small tuft of black wool into a triangle. Felt one end of the beak, creating a point, but leave the fibers loose at the other end. Attach the beak by felting the loose fibers to the head (**refer to page 11**). Insert a small tuft of salmon pink wool into each side of the beak, **as shown in the diagram on the opposite page**.

6. Tail: Form a tuft of black wool into a flat fan shape. Felt one end of the tail, leaving the fibers loose at the other end. Attach the tail by felting the loose fibers to the body (**refer to page 13**).

7. Feet: Form small tufts of black wool into two flat rectangles. Felt to shape the feet, using your needle to create indentations for the toes. Felt to attach the feet to the body.

8. Eyes: Sew a black eye to each side of the head (**refer to page 15**).

Continued on page 114

Project Diagram

ADULT PENGUIN

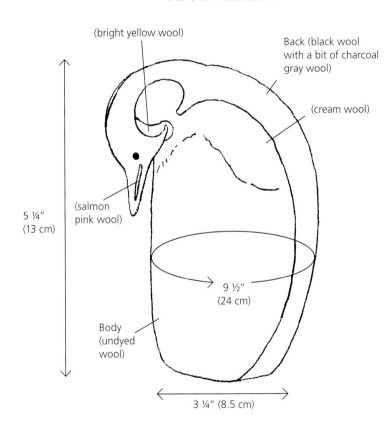

(bright yellow wool)

Back (black wool with a bit of charcoal gray wool)

(cream wool)

(salmon pink wool)

Body (undyed wool)

5 ¼" (13 cm)

9 ½" (24 cm)

3 ¼" (8.5 cm)

Flipper

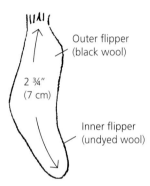

Outer flipper (black wool)

2 ¾" (7 cm)

Inner flipper (undyed wool)

Tail

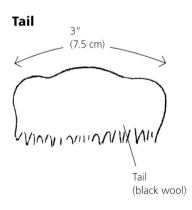

3" (7.5 cm)

Tail (black wool)

Feet

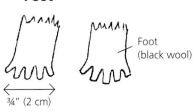

Foot (black wool)

¾" (2 cm)

Emperor Penguins

Materials

BABY PENGUIN
Wool roving:
- 5 g of gray wool
- 3 g of undyed wool
- Small amount of black wool
- Small amount of charcoal gray wool

Instructions

Refer to pages 10–15 for a step-by-step photo reference of general felting and assembly techniques.

BABY PENGUIN

1. Body: Roll a tuft of gray wool into an egg. Felt to shape the body until it is 4 ¾" (12 cm) around the middle.

2. Head: Roll a tuft of undyed wool into a ball and felt into shape. Join the head and body, **as shown on page 12**.

3. Flippers: Form small tufts of gray wool into two flat ovals and felt into shape. Felt to attach a flipper to each side of the body.

4. Markings: Felt black wool to the head, **as shown in the diagram below**.

5. Beak: Form a small tuft of charcoal gray wool into a rectangle. Felt one end of the beak, leaving the fibers loose at the other end. Attach the beak by felting the loose fibers to the head **(refer to page 11)**.

6. Eyes: Felt two thinly curved strips of black wool to the head.

Project Diagram

BABY PENGUIN

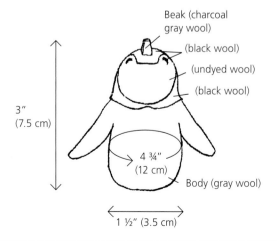

Beak (charcoal gray wool)

(black wool)

(undyed wool)

(black wool)

3" (7.5 cm)

4 ¾" (12 cm)

Body (gray wool)

1 ½" (3.5 cm)

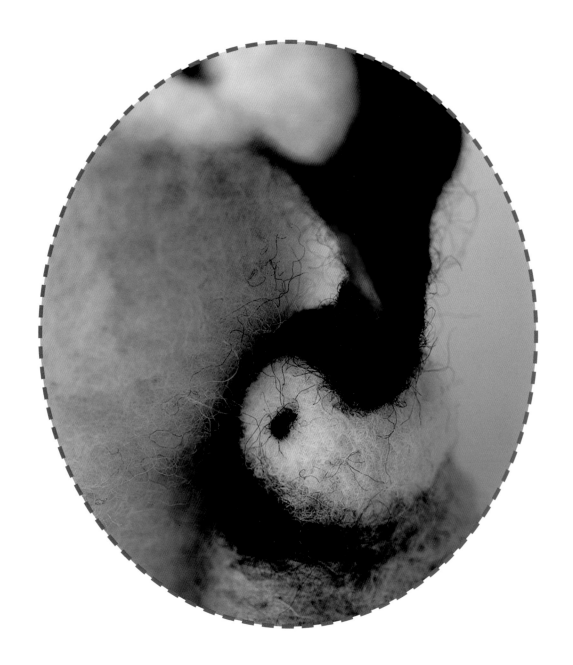

Kangaroos

𝒦angaroos

Materials (for adult and baby)

Wool roving:
- 25 g of beige wool
- 6 g of reddish brown wool
- Small amount of dark brown wool

Eyes:
- Two 6 mm diameter black eyes (for adult)
- Two 4 mm diameter black eyes (for baby)

Refer to pages 10–15 for a step-by-step photo reference of general felting and assembly techniques.

Adult Kangaroo

1. Body: Roll a tuft of beige wool into a cylinder. Felt to shape the body until it is 1½" (4 cm) around the middle. Add wool to the lower body and felt into a rounded shape.

2. Head: Roll a tuft of beige wool into a cone and felt into shape. Use your needle to make an indentation down the center of the head. Join the head and body, **as shown on page 12**.

3. Tail: Roll a small tuft of beige wool into a 2 ¼" (7 cm) long cylinder. Felt one end of the tail, leaving the fibers loose at the other end. Attach the tail by felting the loose fibers to the body (**refer to page 13**).

4. Ears: Roll small tufts of reddish brown wool into two short cylinders. Felt to shape the ears, leaving the fibers loose at one end. Layer a bit of beige wool on top of each ear and felt, concentrating the felting at the center to create a curved shape. Attach ears by felting the loose fibers to the head (**refer to page 12**).

5. Arms: Roll small tufts of beige wool into two thin cylinders. Felt one end of each arm, leaving the fibers loose at the other end. Attach the arms by felting the loose fibers to the body (**refer to page 11**). Bend the arms and felt in place.

6. Legs: To create the haunches, felt small tufts of beige wool into two circles and attach to the body. Roll small tufts of beige wool into two thin cylinders. Felt one end of each leg, leaving the fibers loose at the other end. Attach the legs by felting the loose fibers to the haunches (**refer to page 11**). To create the feet, bend the legs and felt into place.

Continued on page 120

Tip:
Make the adult's legs and tail thick in order to hold the body upright.

Project Diagram

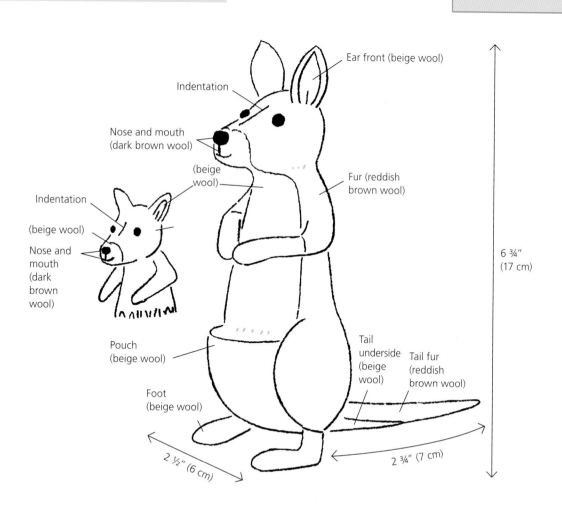

Ear front (beige wool)

Indentation

Nose and mouth (dark brown wool)

(beige wool)

Fur (reddish brown wool)

Indentation

(beige wool)

Nose and mouth (dark brown wool)

Pouch (beige wool)

Foot (beige wool)

Tail underside (beige wool)

Tail fur (reddish brown wool)

6 ¾" (17 cm)

2 ½" (6 cm)

2 ¾" (7 cm)

Baby Kangaroo

1. Body: Roll a small tuft of beige wool into a cylinder. Felt to shape the body, leaving the fibers loose at one end.

2. Head and Ears: Repeat step 2 to make the baby's head and step 4 to make the baby's ears.

3. Arms: Repeat step 3 to make the baby's arms, using reddish brown wool.

Finish the Kangaroos

1. Attach: Join the baby to the adult by felting the loose fibers of the baby's body to the underside of the adult's body. To make the pouch, position a piece of beige wool on top of the baby's body. Felt to attach the wool to the underside of the adult's body. Felt reddish brown wool to the adult, leaving the underside of the body, underside of the tail, lower arms, feet, and nose visible. Felt reddish brown wool to baby's head, leaving the nose visible.

2. Finish: To make each nose, roll a tiny ball of dark brown wool between your fingertips and felt to attach to the head. To make each mouth, felt two thin strips of dark brown wool to the head, directly beneath the nose. Sew the black eyes to each head (**refer to page 15**).